THIS AMERICAN MILITARY COLORING BOOK BELONGS TO:

_____

D.O.G. PUBLISHING

Copyright © 2022 by Dale O. Garrett and D.O.G. Publishing
All rights reserved. No portion of this book may be reproduced in any form without
The express written consent of the publisher, except as permitted by U.S. copyright laws.
PROUDLY CREATED BY AN AMERICAN.
PRINTED, AND MAUFACTURED IN THE UNITED STATES OF AMERICA

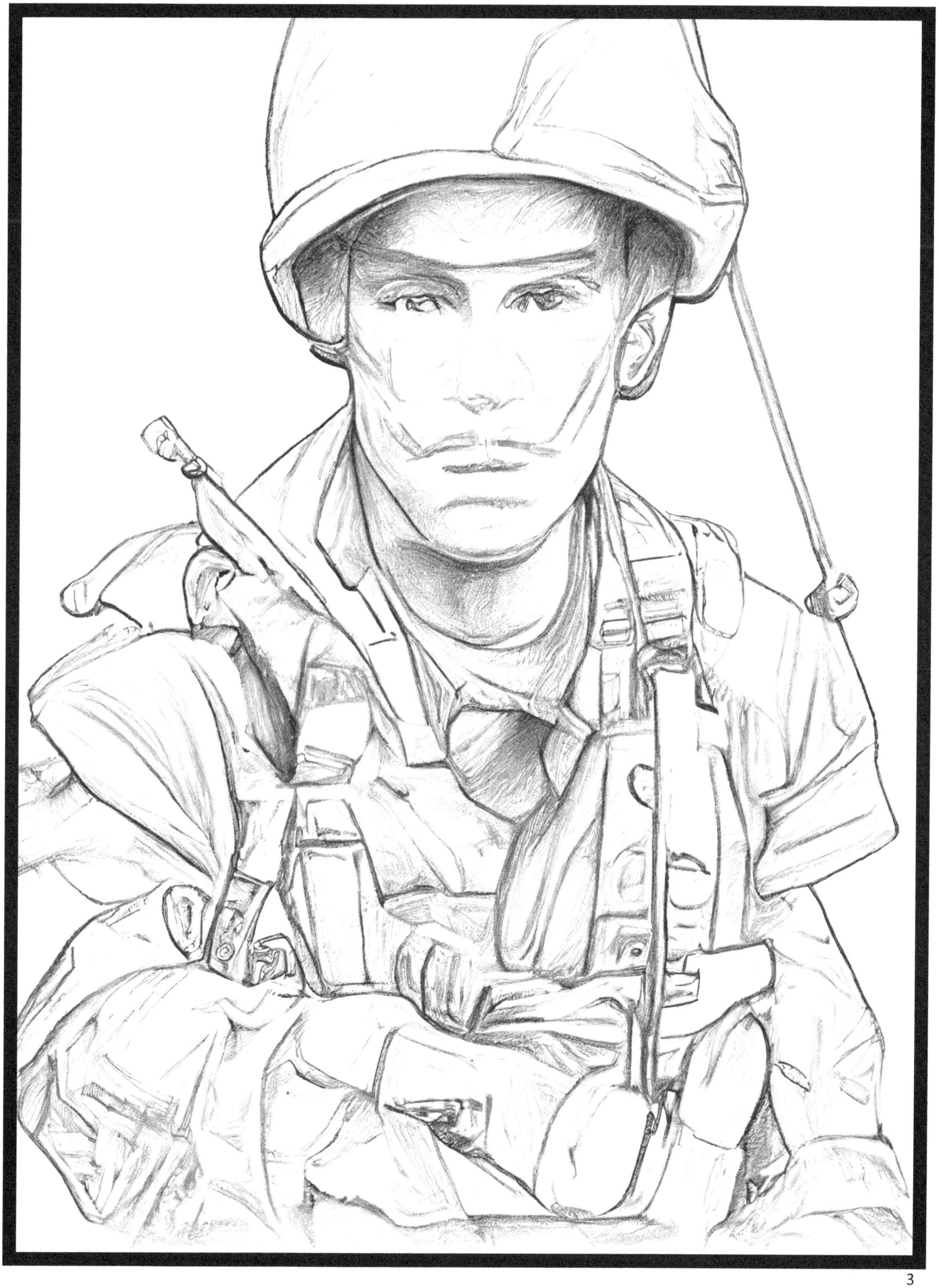

5

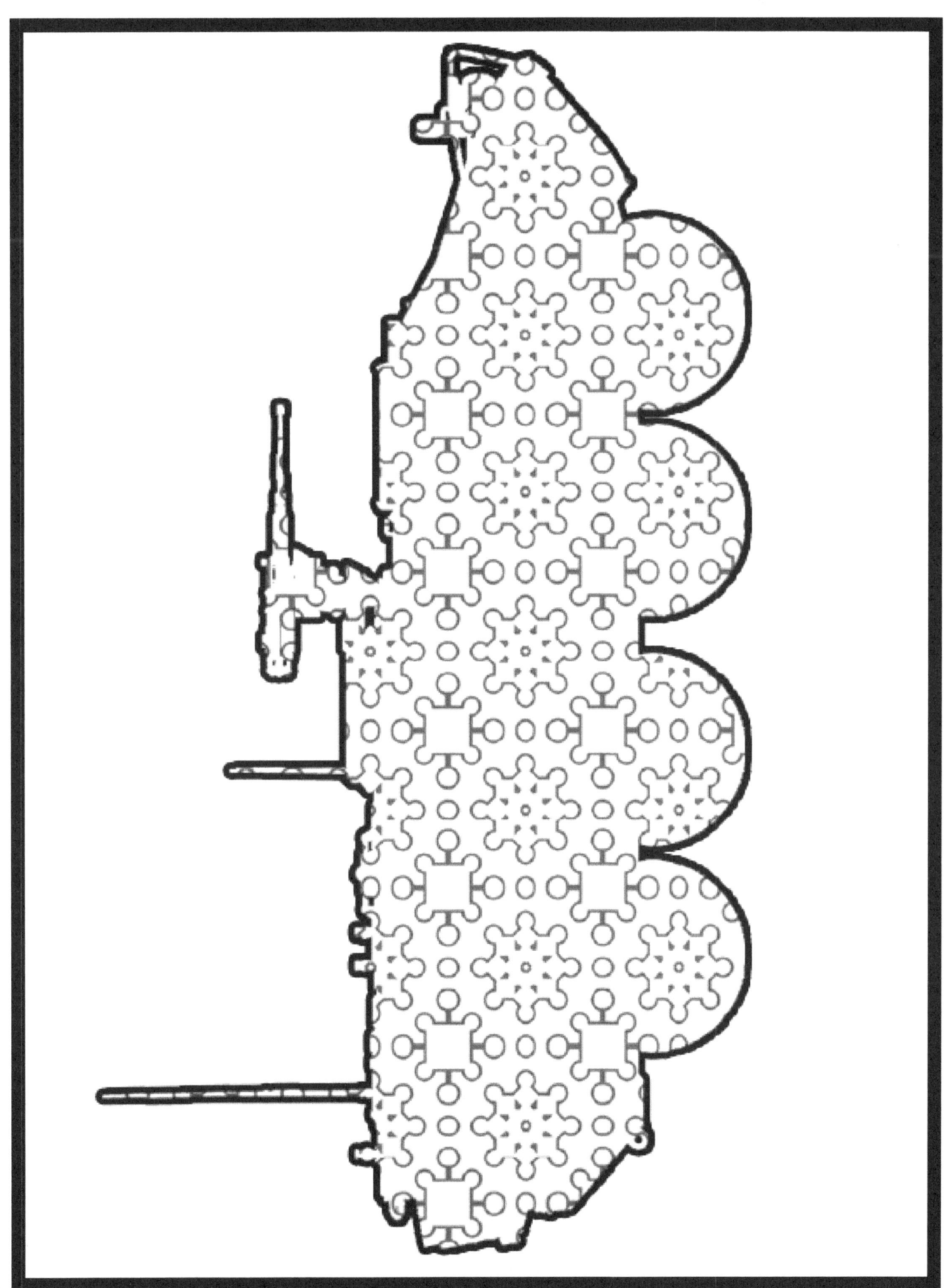

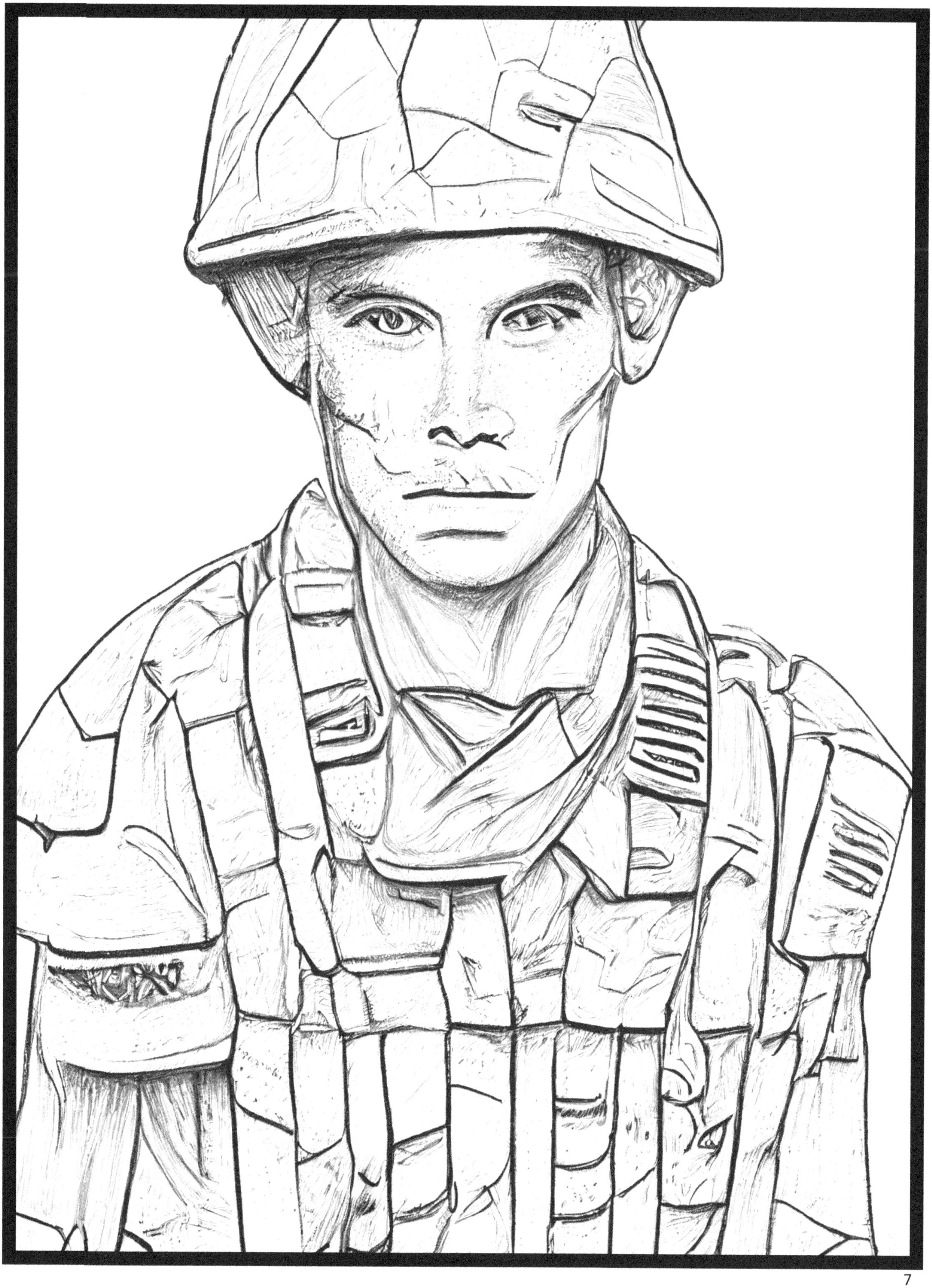

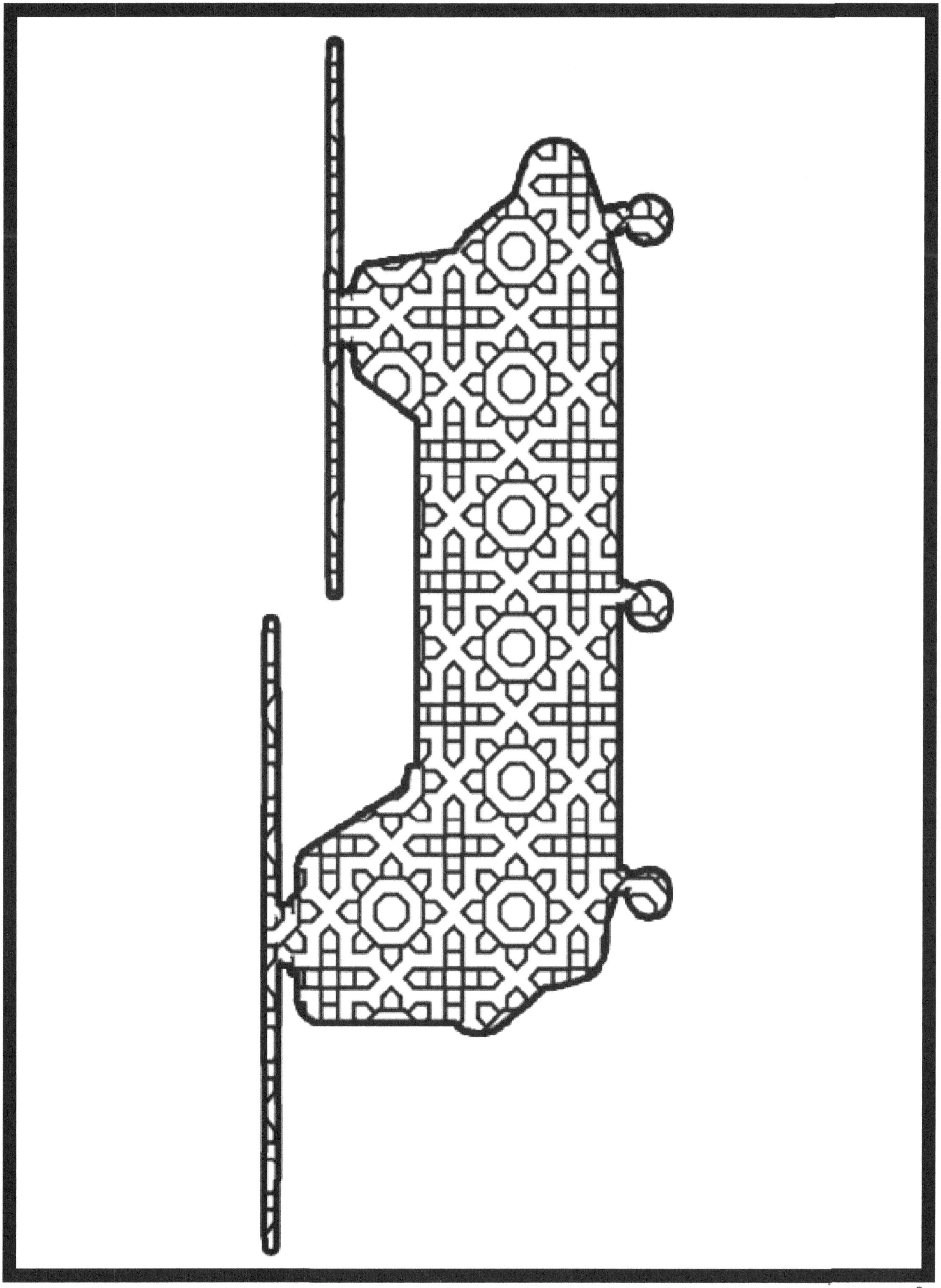

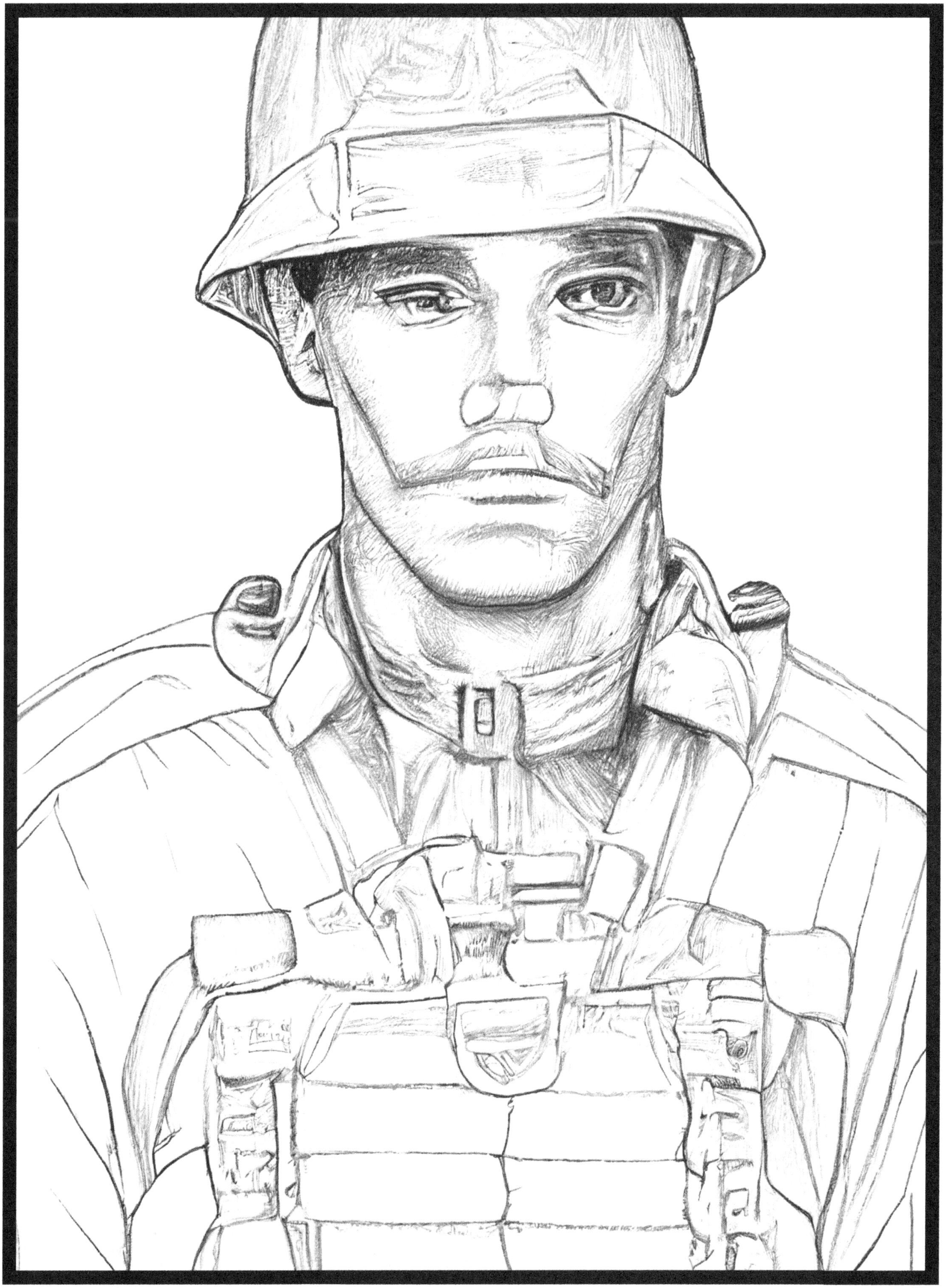

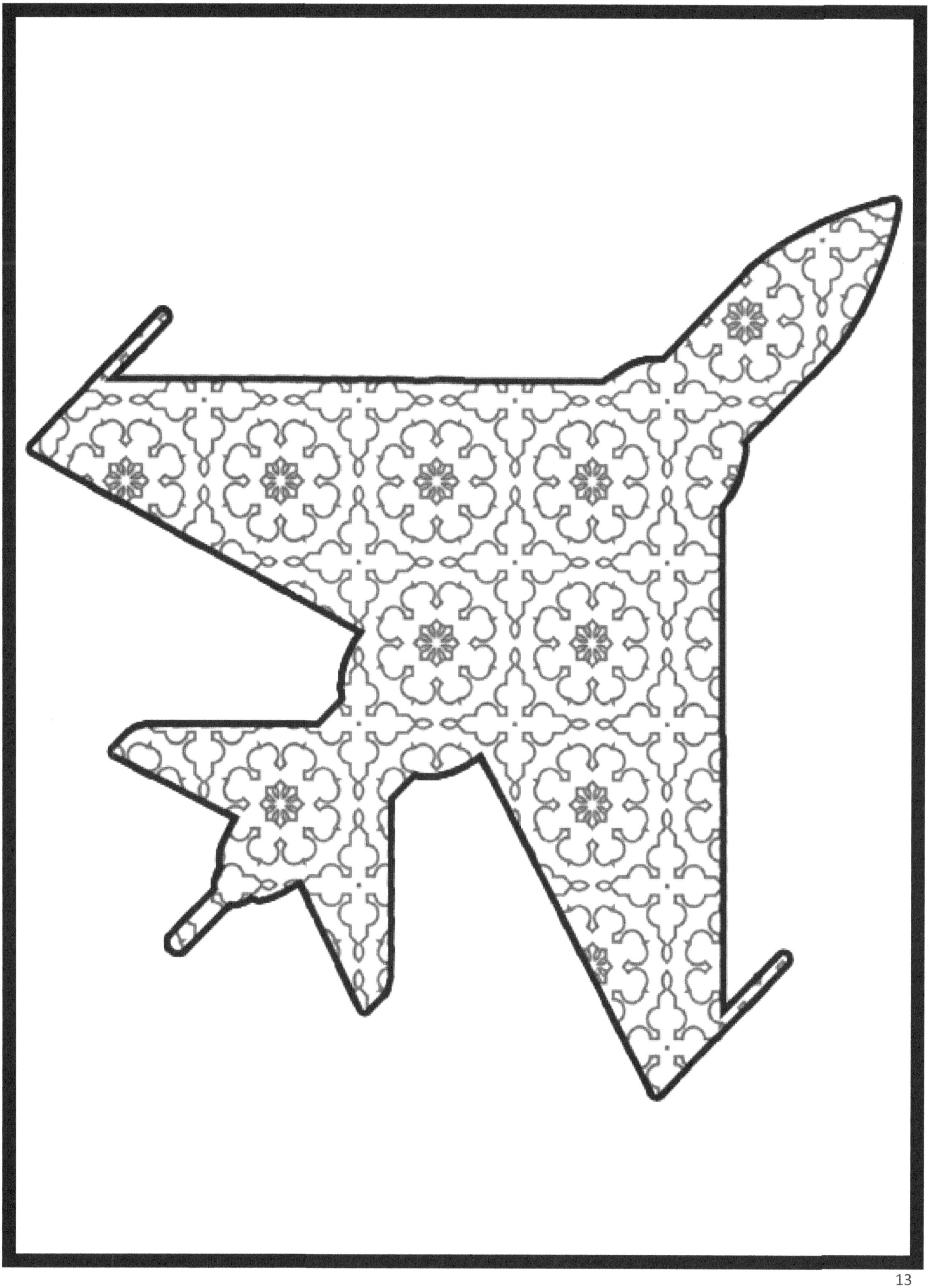

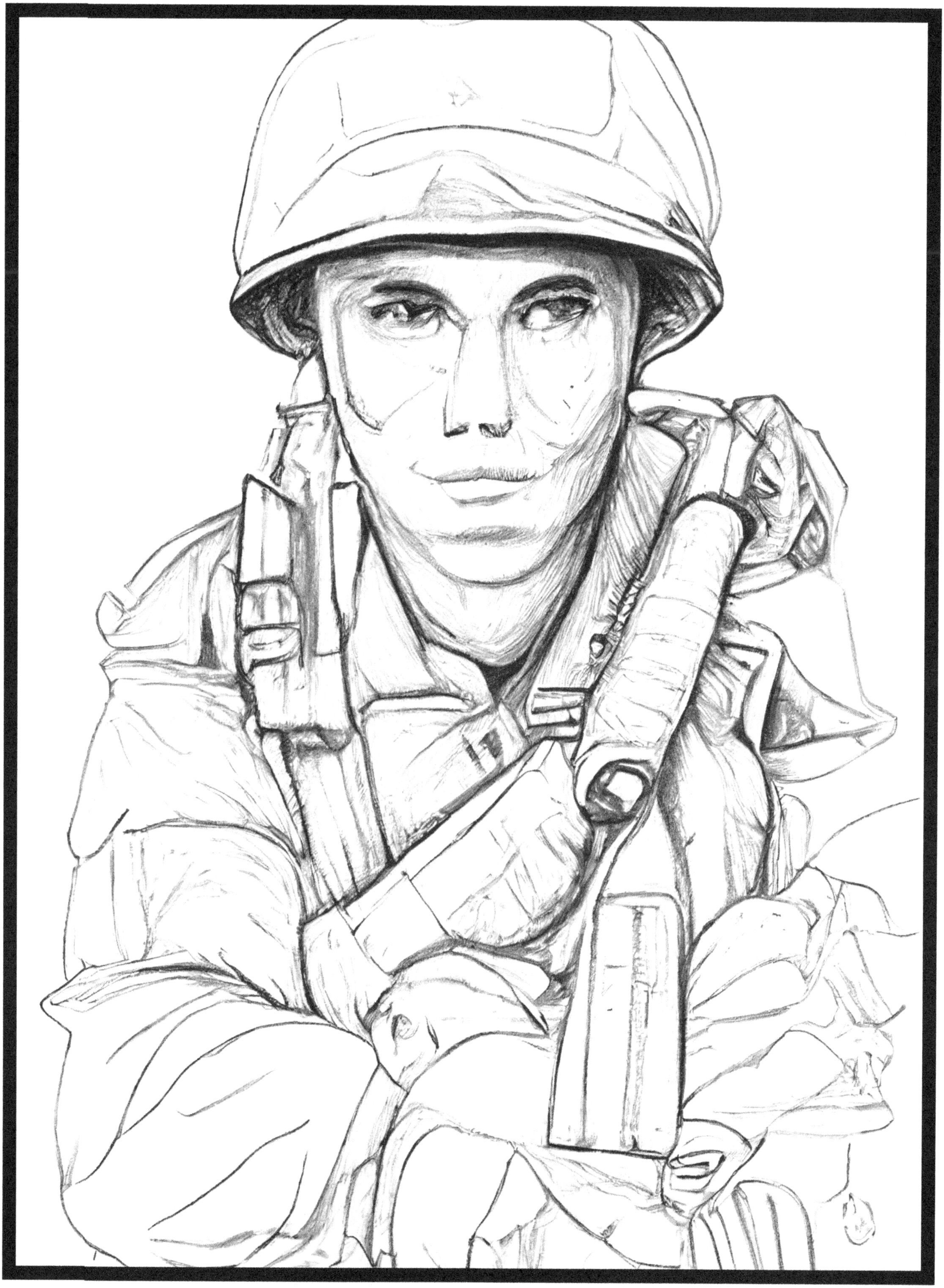

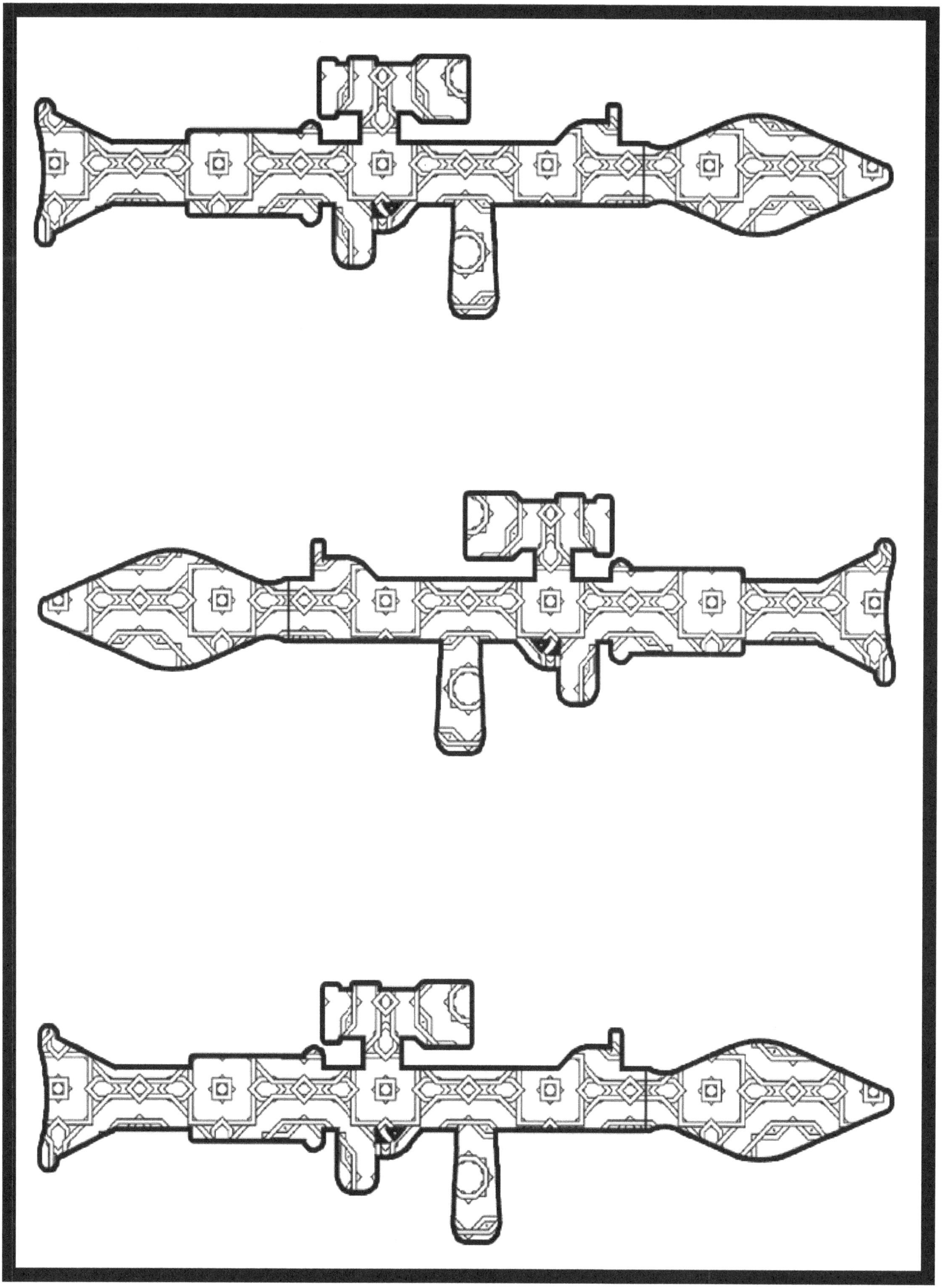

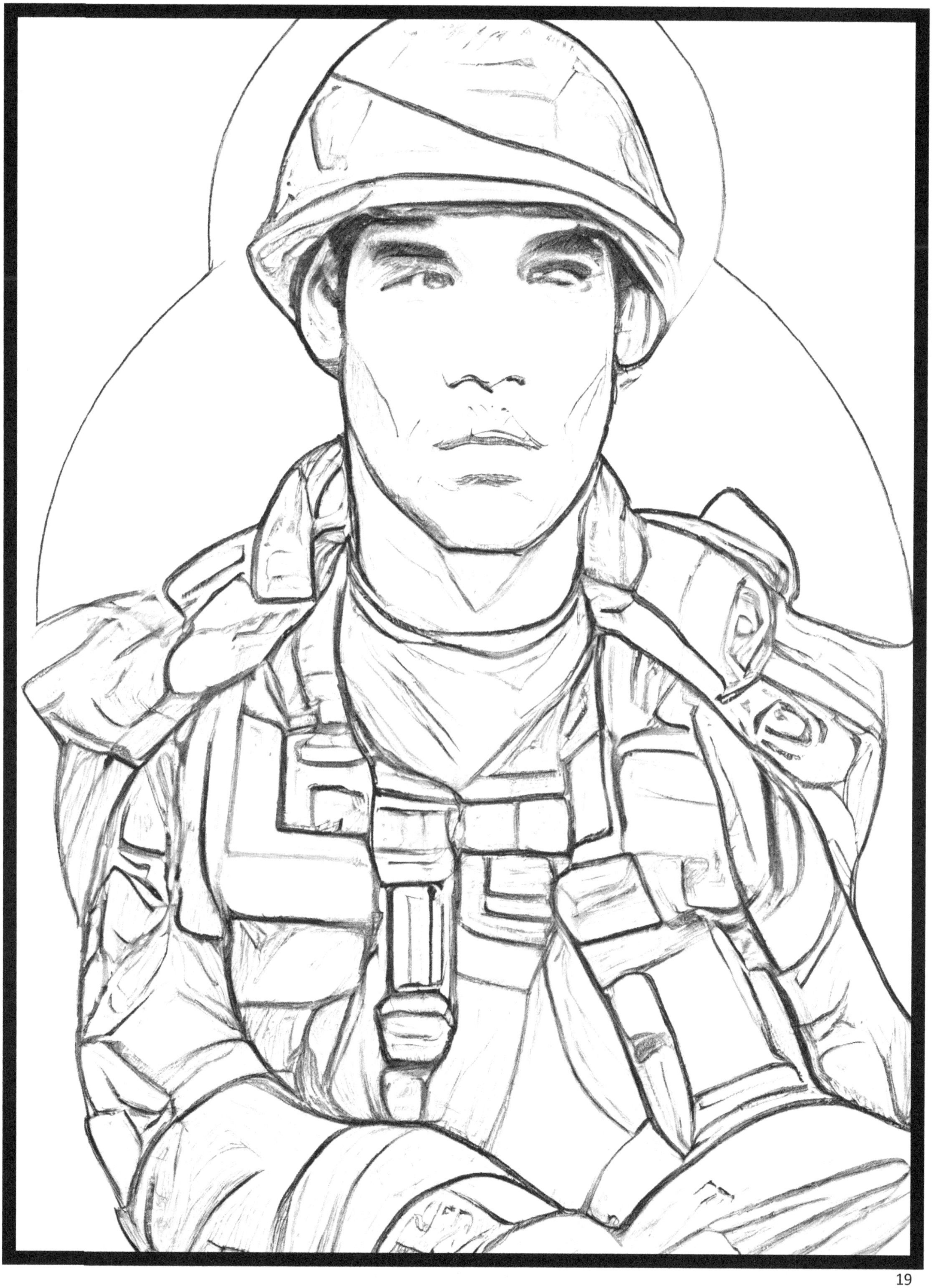

21

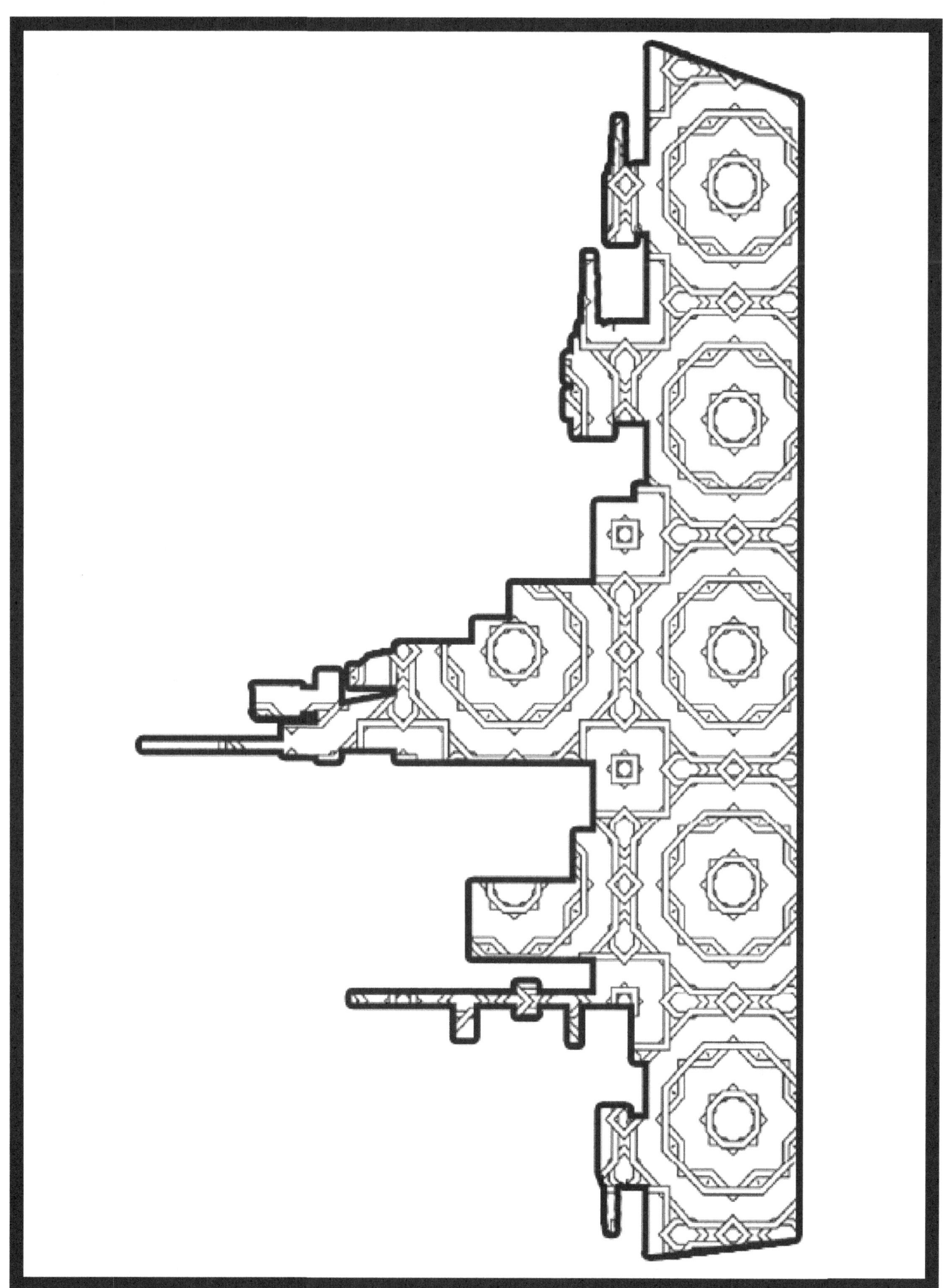

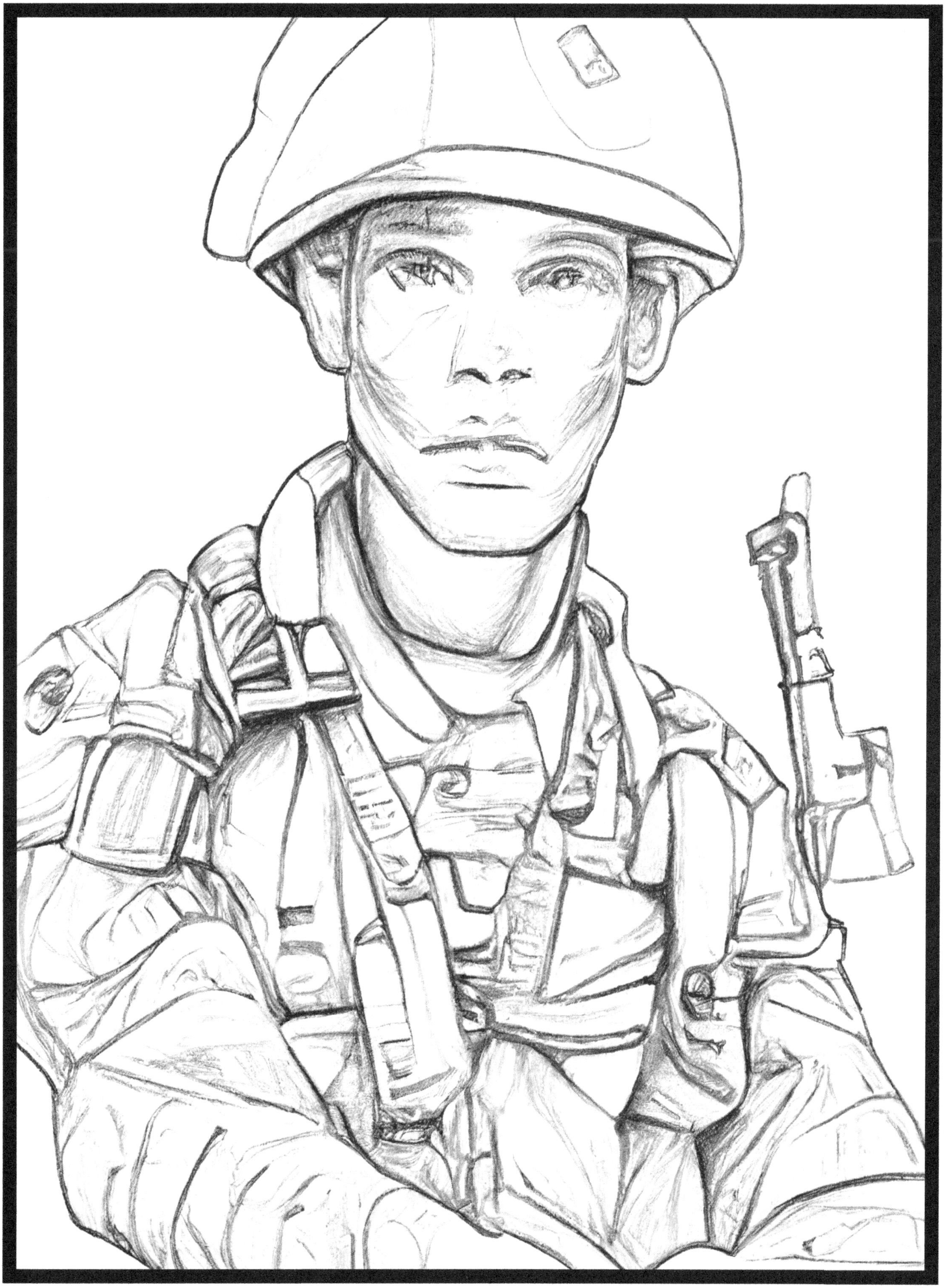

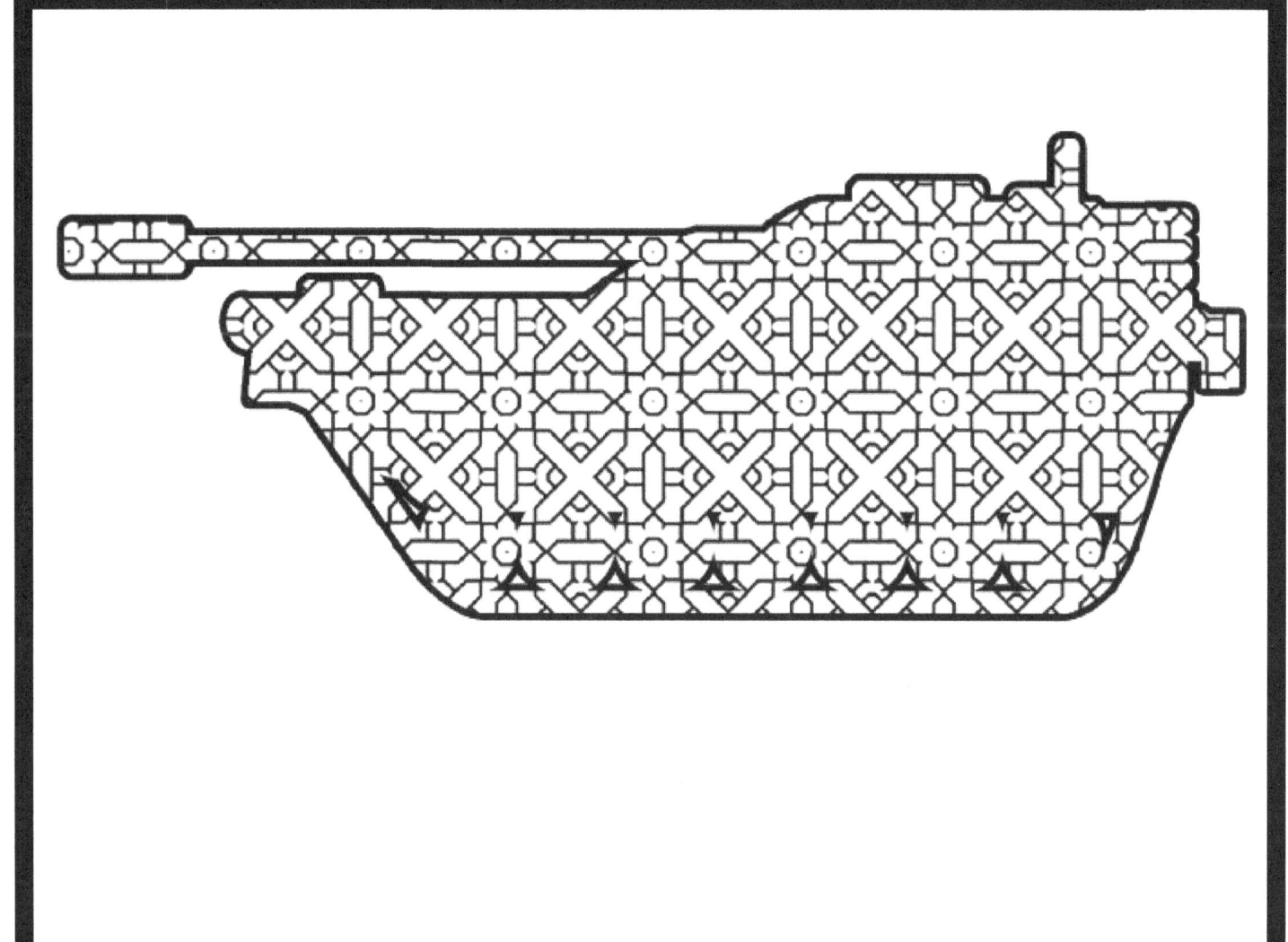

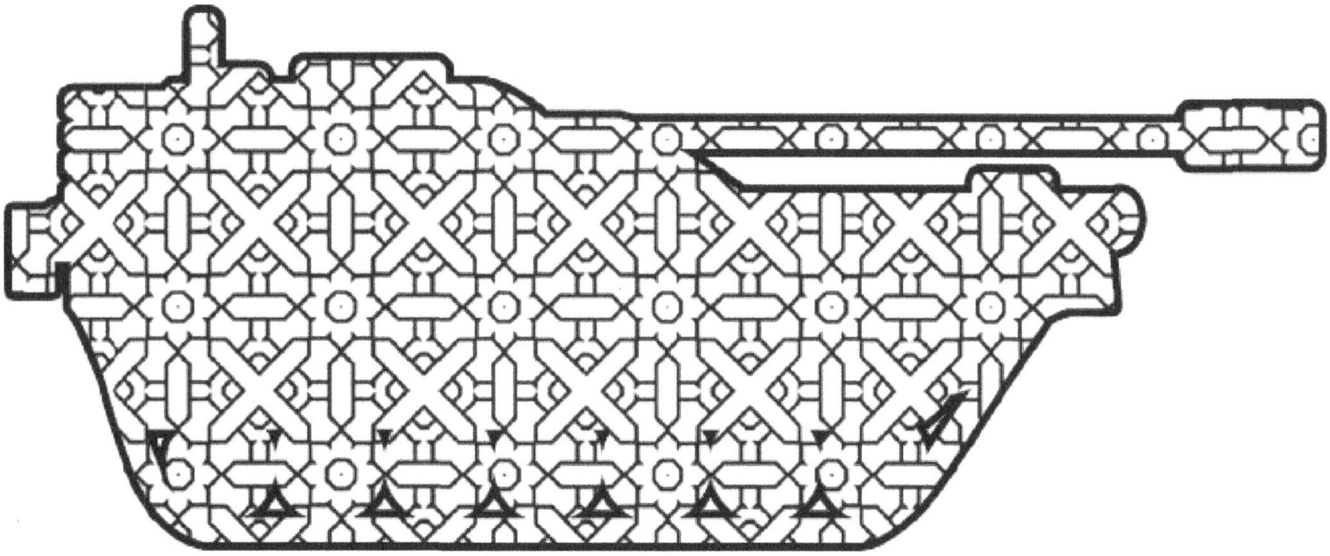

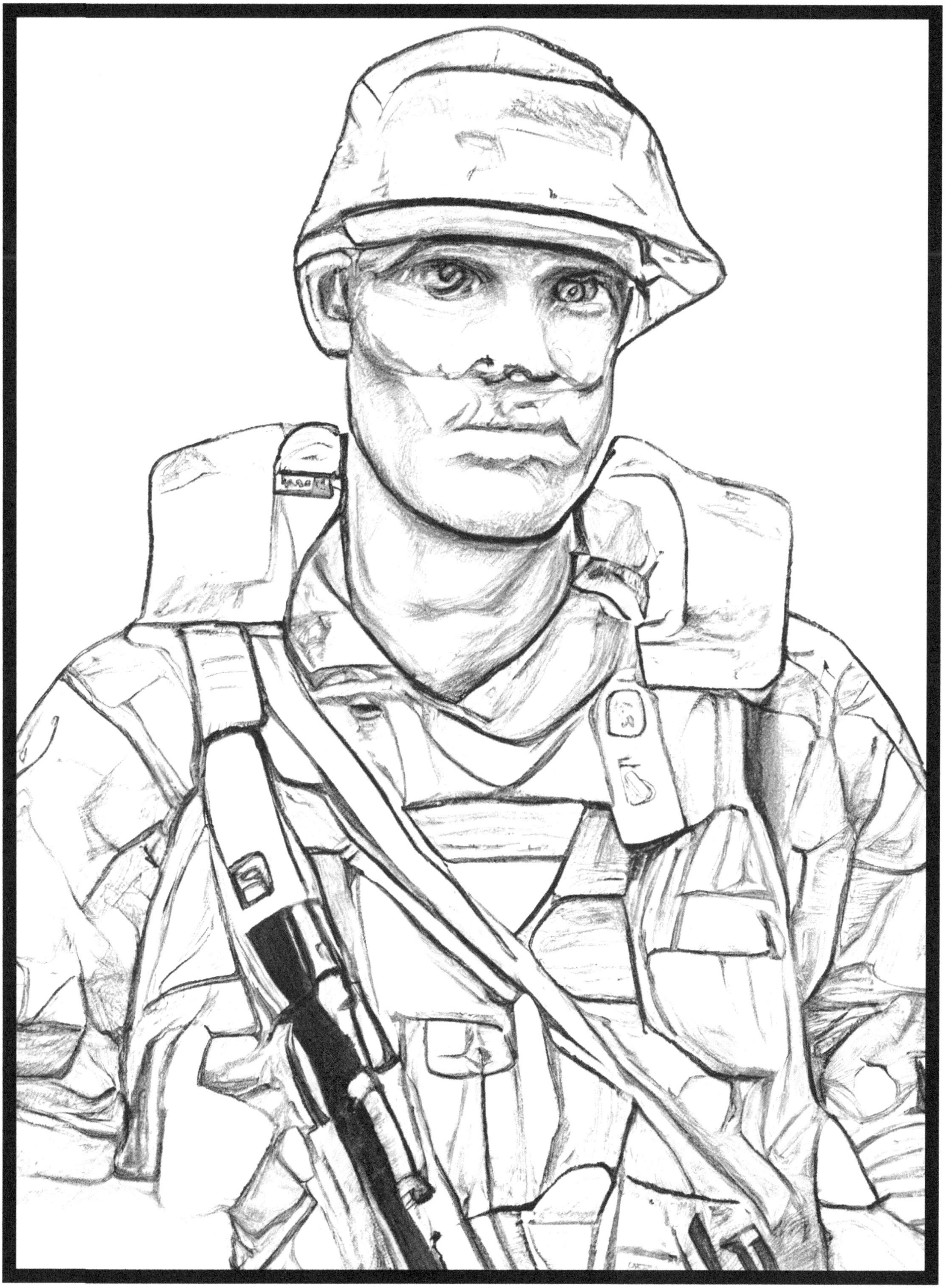

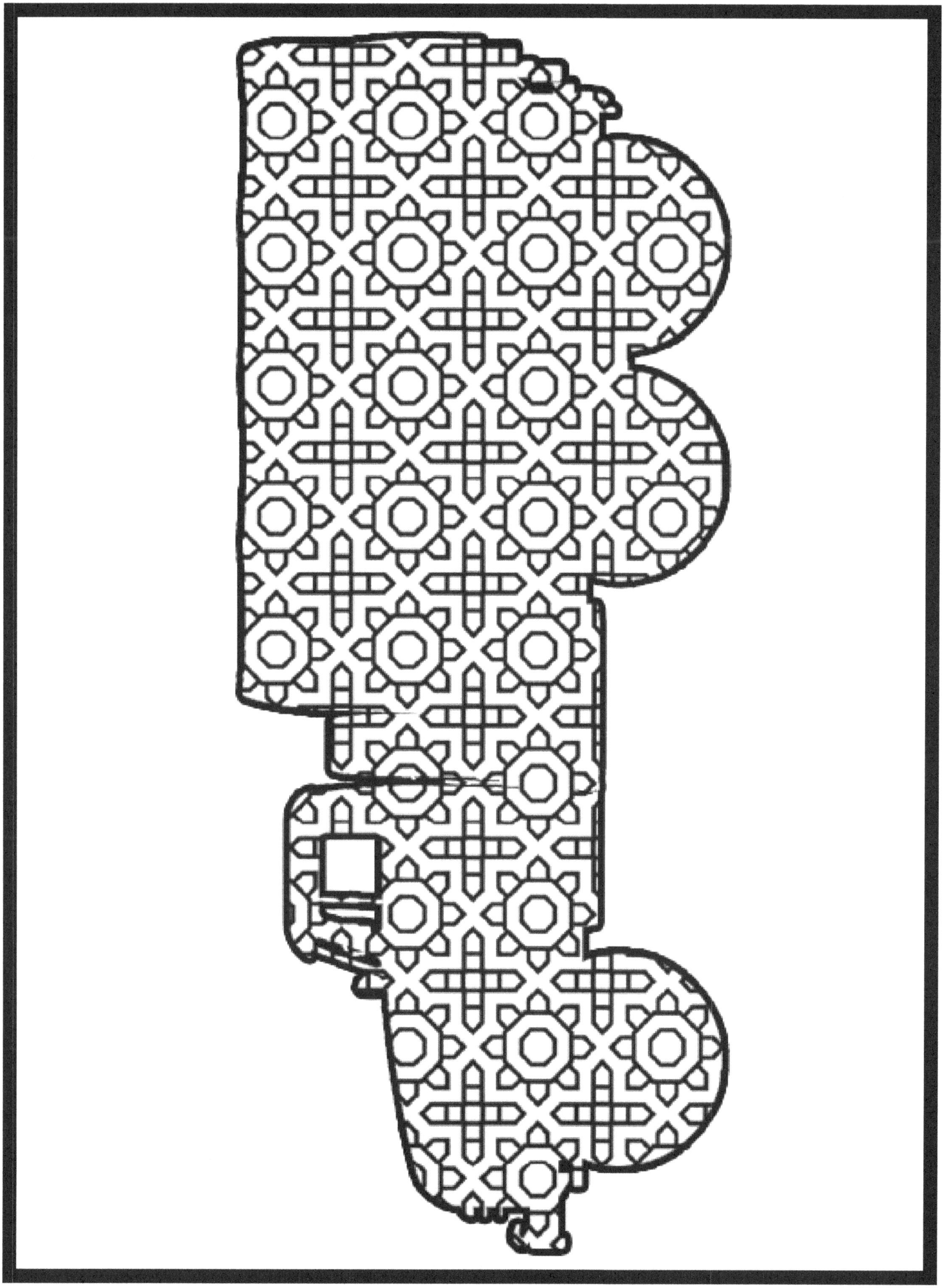

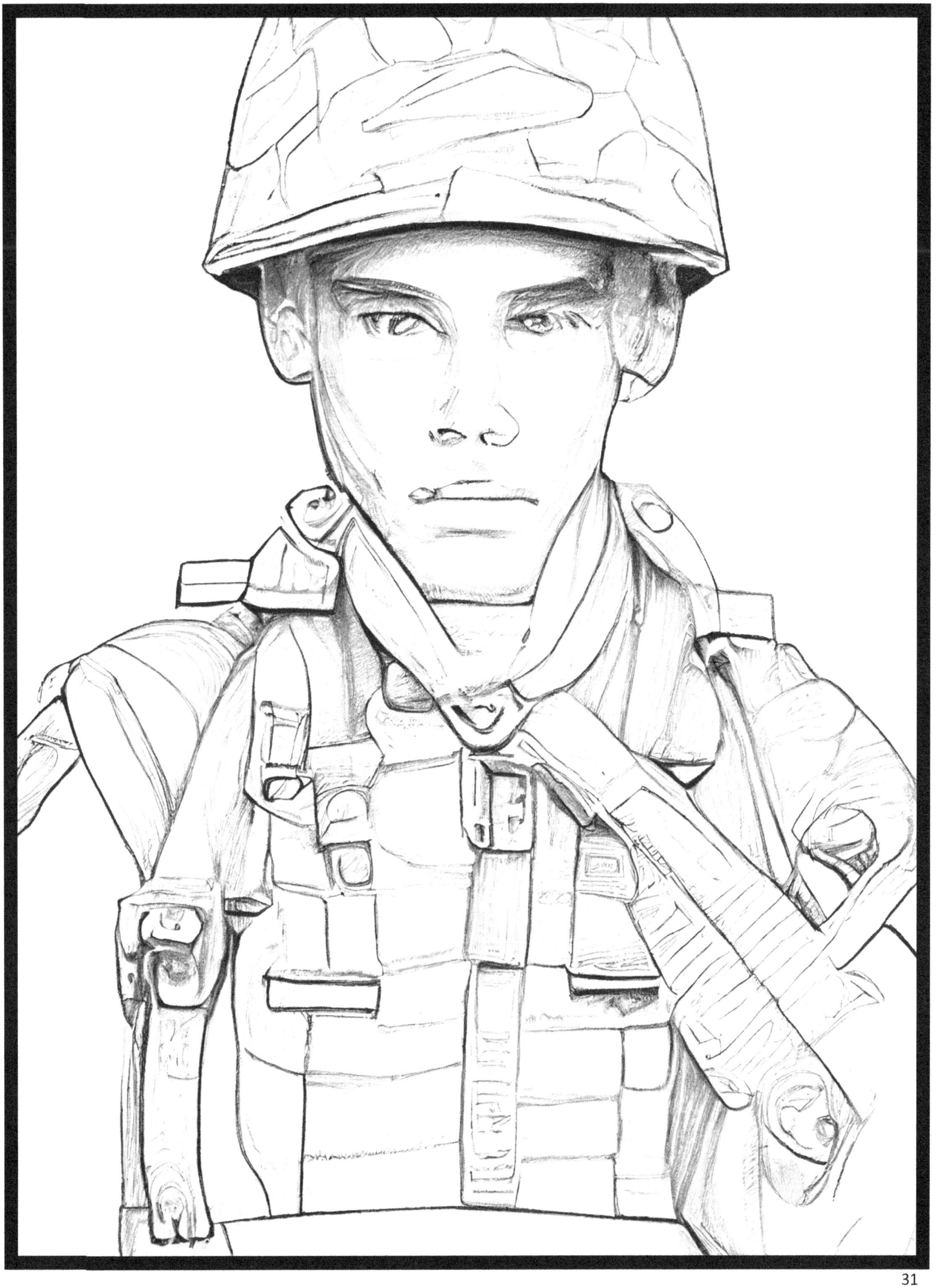

33

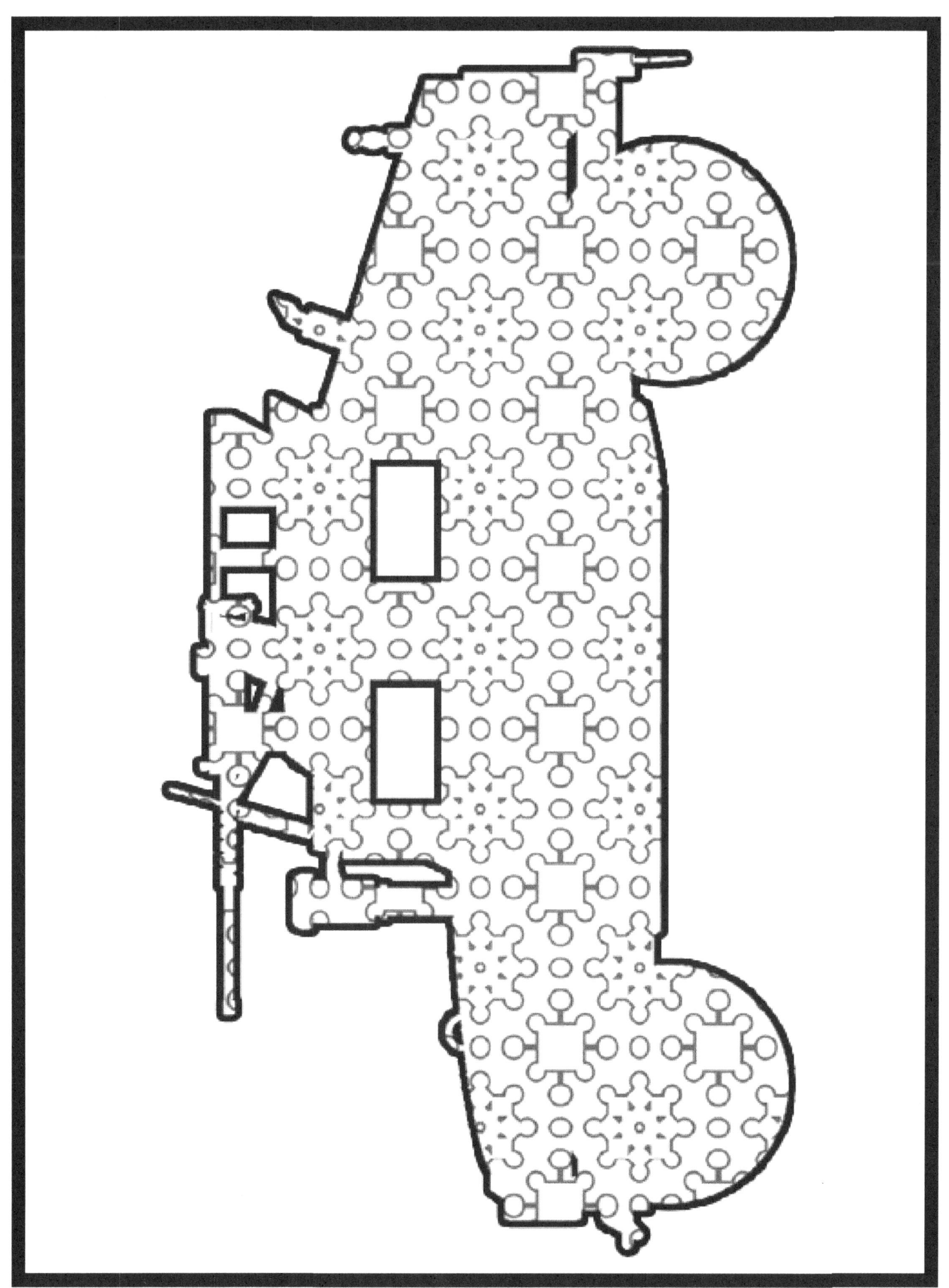

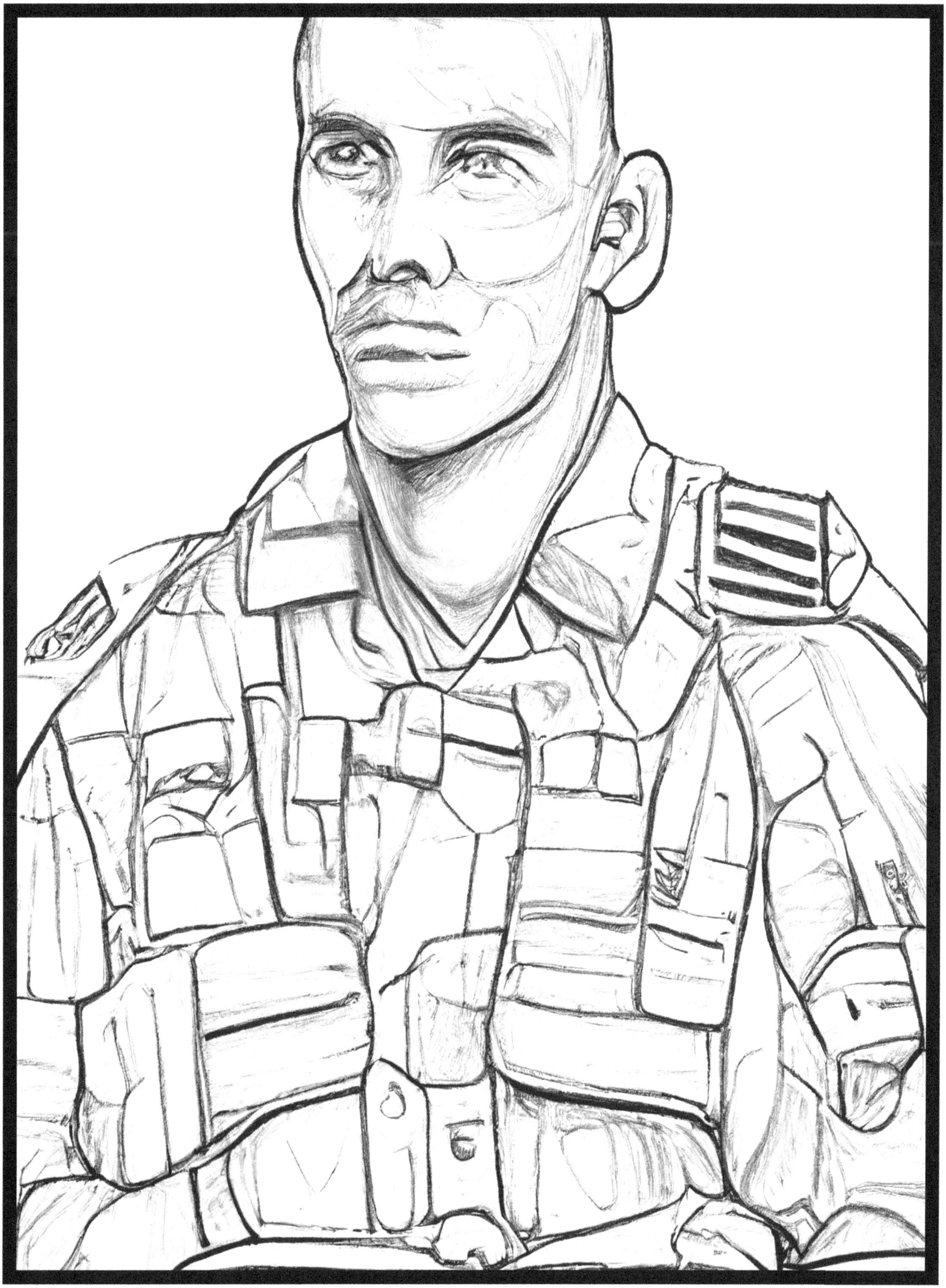

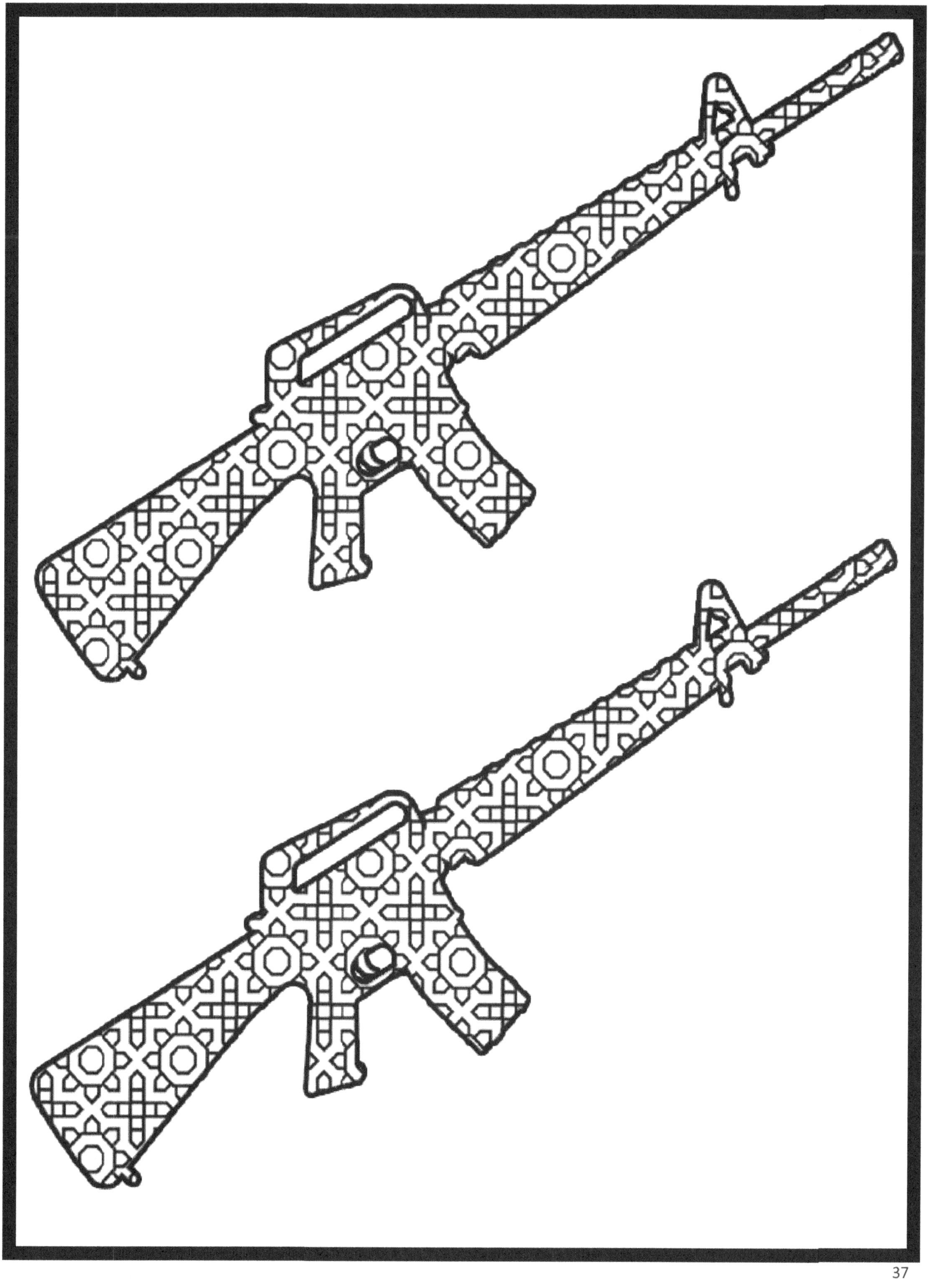

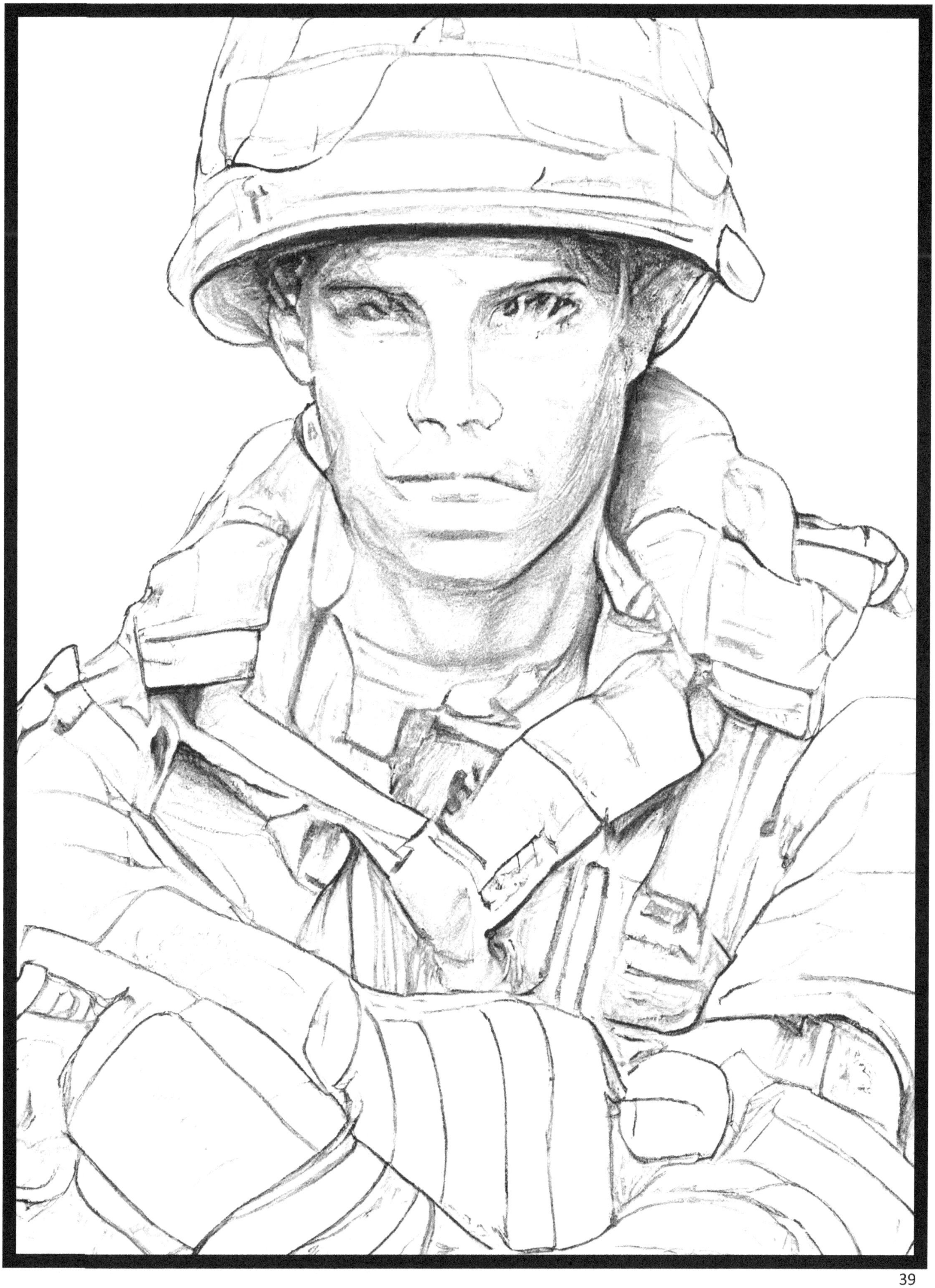

41

D.O.G. PUBLISHING

For more books by this author, scan the below QR code with your mobile phone or, visit:
https://www.amazon.com/~/e/B0B1YY6PSY

Made in the USA
Columbia, SC
07 January 2023